MEXICANS

IMMIGRATION AND THE AMERICAN WAY OF LIFE

Geologically speaking, the continent of North America is very old. The people who live here, by comparison, are new arrivals. Even the first settlers, the American Indians who came here from Asia about 35,000 years ago, are fairly new, not to speak of the first European settlers who came by ship or the refugees who flew in yesterday. Whenever they came, they were all immigrants. How all these immigrants live together today to form one society has been compared to the making of a mosaic. A mosaic is a picture formed from many different pieces. Thus, in America, many groups of people—from African Americans or Albanians to Tibetans or Welsh—live side by side. This human mosaic was put together by the immigrants themselves, with courage, hard work, and luck. Each group of immigrants has its own history and its own reasons for coming to America. Immigrants from different regions have their own way of creating communities for themselves and their children. In creating those communities, they not only keep elements of their own heritage alive, but also enrich further the fabric of American society. Each book in *Recent American Immigrants* will examine a part of this human mosaic up close. The books will look at some of the most recent arrivals to find out what they are like and how they fit into the whole mosaic.

Recent American Immigrants

MEXICANS

Jodine Mayberry

Consultant
Roger Daniels, Department of History
University of Cincinnati

Franklin Watts
New York • London • Toronto • Sydney

Developed by: Ω Visual Education Corporation
Princeton, NJ

Cover Photograph: Bob Daemmrich/The Image Works

Photo Credits: p. 3 (L) Craig Aurness/Woodfin Camp & Associates:
p. 3 (M) Bob Daemmrich/The Image Works; p. 3 (R) Ellis Herwig/
Stock, Boston; p. 10 Alon Reininger/Woodfin Camp & Associates;
p. 11 North Wind Picture Archives; p. 12 North Wind Picture
Archives; p. 13 The New-York Historical Society; p. 17 North Wind
Picture Archives; p. 18 Culver Pictures, Inc.; p. 20 UPI/Bettmann
Newsphotos; p. 24 The Institute of Texan Cultures; p. 25 The Institute
of Texan Cultures; p. 26 Security Pacific National Bank Photograph
Collection/Los Angeles Public Library; p. 28 Security Pacific
National Bank Photograph Collection/Los Angeles Public Library;
p. 32 The Institute of Texan Cultures; p. 35 Bob Daemmrich/The
Image Works; p. 36 Alon Reininger/Woodfin Camp & Associates;
p. 39 Dan McCoy/Rainbow; p. 42 Gerhard Gscheidle/Peter Arnold,
Inc.; p. 44 UPI/Bettmann Newsphotos; p. 46 Bob Daemmrich/The
Image Works; p. 50 Cynthia Johnson/Gamma-Liaison; p. 51
Stephanie Maze/Woodfin Camp & Associates; p. 52 Arizona
Department of Library, Archives and Public Records; p. 53 Pam
Price/Picture Group; p. 54 Culver Pictures, Inc.; p. 55 Christiana
Dittmann/Rainbow; p. 57 J. Brenner/FPG International; p. 58 (L)
D. Donne Bryant/FPG International; p. 58 (R) Stan Sholik/FPG
International; p. 61 Jay Lurie/FPG International

Library of Congress Cataloging-in-Publication Data

Mayberry, Jodine, 1946-
Mexicans/Jodine Mayberry
p.   cm. — (Recent American immigrants)
Includes bibliographical references (p.   ).
Summary: Discusses Mexicans who have immigrated to the United States,
their reasons for coming, their lifestyles, and their
contributions to their new country.
ISBN 0-531-10979-8
1. Mexican Americans — Juvenile literature. 2. United States — Emigration
and immigration — Juvenile literature. 3. Mexico — Emigration and
immigration — Juvenile literature. 4. [1. Mexican Americans.] I. Title.
II. Series: Recent American immigrants.
E184.M5G65   1990
973′.046872073 — dc20   90-32095 CIP AC

Contents

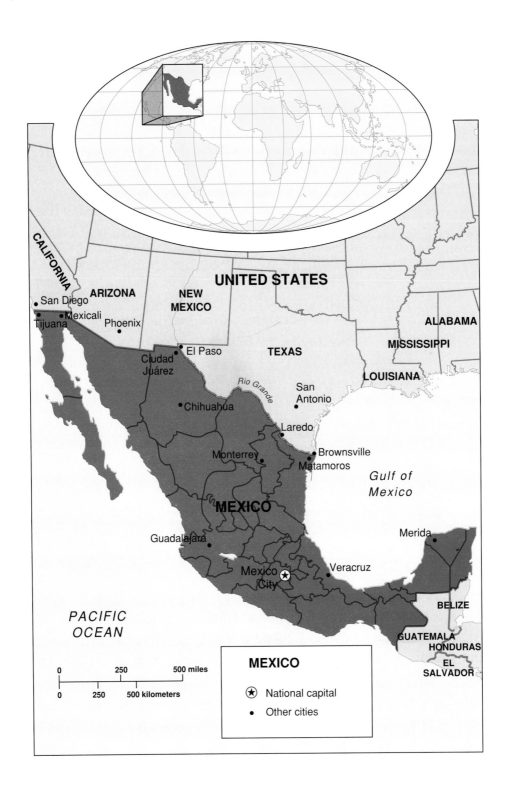

CALIFORNIA

ARIZONA

NEW
MEXICO

UNITED STATES

ALABAMA

MISSISSIPPI

San Diego

Mexicali

Tijuana

Phoenix

El Paso

TEXAS

LOUISIANA

Ciudad
Juárez

Rio Grande

San
Antonio

Chihuahua

Laredo

Monterrey

Brownsville

Matamoros

Gulf of
Mexico

MEXICO

Merida

Guadalajara

Mexico
City

Veracruz

BELIZE

PACIFIC
OCEAN

GUATEMALA

HONDURAS

EL
SALVADOR

0   250   500 miles

0   250   500 kilometers

MEXICO

⭐ National capital

• Other cities

6

The Creation of the Mexican American Community, 1513–1900

MEXICO

Mexico is America's next-door neighbor to the south. It shares a 2,000-mile border with the United States. Mexico is a rugged land of deserts, mountains, and jungles. Most people are farmers, but many work in offices and factories. Most people in Mexico are poor. They live in small villages or in slums surrounding the big cities.

Mexico's population is growing very fast. In 1989, it had a population of about 89 million people. By the year 2000, it is expected to have 109 million people. Mexico has never been able to provide enough land or jobs for all of its people. In 1848, Mexico lost a huge amount of land to the United States. Since early in the twentieth century, many Mexicans have been looking for work in the United States. They can make more money here than in Mexico. They send money home to support their families. Often, their families come with them and work as well. In the United States, farmers and factory owners seek workers who will labor for low wages. They often hire Mexicans for these jobs.

Because the United States is so close, it has always been easy for Mexicans (and Canadians) to immigrate to the United States. European and Asian immigrants have to cross thousands of miles of water. Mexicans need only walk or drive across the border. Much of the land along the Mexican-American border is open, barren desert. This has made it very difficult for the United States to stop Mexicans from coming in.

Mexican Americans are among America's oldest immigrants. In Santa Fe and elsewhere in New Mexico, you can find Mexican American families whose ancestors settled there early in the 1600s. Mexicans are also among America's newest immigrants. In border towns like El Paso, Texas, and Nogales, Arizona, you can find Mexicans who arrived only yesterday or last week. Like so many other immigrants, Mexicans see America as a land of opportunity. To them, it is a place where they can live better lives and provide more for their children.

MEXICO'S EARLY HISTORY

Like the United States, Mexico was first populated by Indians. The Indian tribes of Mexico developed into two great civilizations. The Mayas flourished from about A.D. 500 to 900. They built large cities throughout Mexico and Central America. They devised a form of writing and created an accurate calendar.

For some unknown reason, the Maya civilization disappeared. Then the Aztecs came to central Mexico around A.D. 1300. They were very warlike. They defeated the surrounding tribes and built a large empire. The Aztecs built a beautiful capital city in the middle of a lake, where Mexico City now stands. The capital was named Tenochtitlán.

In 1519, Hernando Cortés, a Spanish conquistador (soldier and explorer), arrived in Mexico. He brought about 500 soldiers and horses and guns. Within a few months, Cortés brutally conquered the Aztecs and brought their empire to an end.

The successful invasion by the Spanish brought enormous changes to Mexico. The Spanish enslaved the Indians to work in gold and silver mines and on large agricultural estates they seized. Spanish priests forcibly converted Indians to Christianity and made them speak Spanish. Since few women came from Spain, most Spanish men married Indian women. Their children, part Spanish and part Indian, were called *mestizos*. The great majority of today's Mexicans are mestizos. Their language and some of the rest of their culture are Spanish. Much of their culture stems from their Indian ancestry.

MEXICO EXPANDS

After they settled in Mexico, the conquistadores kept hearing fables about cities of gold and rich Indian tribes to the north. Francisco Vásquez de Coronado set out in 1540 to search northern Mexico for seven mythical cities of gold. On the way, he explored much of what is now Arizona, New Mexico, Texas, and Kansas. Thirty years later, Juan de Onate led a small group of Spanish colonists into New Mexico. The colonists brought horses and cattle with them. The horses multiplied into large herds of wild mustangs that later roamed the western plains. The cattle were the ancestors of the Texas longhorn cattle.

California Missions In 1542, Spanish explorers sailed up the coast of California but made no permanent settlement. Two centuries later, Father Junipero Serra, a Franciscan missionary, built a mission at San Diego on the southern California coast. By the end of the eighteenth century, a string of Catholic missions had been established all along the coast of California.

Mission San Carlos Borromeo at Carmel, California, founded in 1770

The Indians in California were treated much like the ones in Mexico. The missionaries converted them to Christianity and forced them to grow crops, tend cattle, and tan leather. The missions became the centers of Spanish Mexican California. Villages grew up around them and became trading centers. Many Spanish settlers became rich and developed large ranches near the villages.

New Mexican Ranches The Spanish also colonized what is present-day New Mexico. There, the center of settlements was the *presidio,* the Spanish word for "fort." Soldiers were stationed at the presidios to protect the priests and settlers from hostile Indians.

Trade Routes The Spanish established two important trade routes in the Southwest, the old Spanish Trail from Santa Fe to Los Angeles and the Santa Fe Trail from Independence, Missouri, to Santa Fe. Many non-Spanish colonists would later come from the eastern part of the United States to California over these trails or by ship.

Life in California and New Mexico Most of the Spanish colonists who came to Mexico settled in the central and southern parts of the country. Very few went to California or New Mexico, and the Spanish Mexican ranches there were very isolated from one another. The landowners and their workers made or raised most of the products they needed. They built Spanish-style houses, called *haciendas,* of adobe clay. Life in the haciendas included Spanish music and fiestas (feasts), bullfights, and religious holidays.

What They Called Themselves The Spanish settlers in these areas had a variety of names for themselves. Those who lived in California called themselves *Californios.* Those who settled in Texas were *Tejanos.* Generally, they referred to themselves as *Hispanos* or *Mexicanos.* Spanish speakers in the Southwest tended to call persons from the United States *gringos* or *Americanos.* In the twentieth century, they tend to call all non-Spanish speakers *Anglos.* At the same time, a new term came into use for Mexican Americans, *Chicanos.* The origin of that word is not definite. Some Mexican Americans consider the term derogatory. Many others are proud to call themselves Chicanos.

A typical hacienda on a Spanish Mexican ranch in the early 1800s

THE AMERICANOS ARRIVE

In 1821, the people of Mexico won their independence from Spain after a long struggle. At that time, northern Mexico was still very thinly populated. The new Mexican government needed more settlers to help control unfriendly Indian tribes. Mexico invited people from the United States to settle in Texas. Thousands of Americans came to Texas. Many brought their slaves to help farm the new land, although slavery was illegal in Mexico.

The Mexican government gave the new settlers free land. In exchange, Mexico required that the Americans become Mexican citizens. They had to agree to obey Mexican laws (including the law against slavery) and to learn to speak Spanish. Mexico also required them to adopt Catholicism as their religion. By 1834, more than 20,000 Americans had settled in Texas. Only about 5,000 Mexicans lived there.

On to California At the same time that Americans were moving to Texas, other American settlers were arriving by ship in northern California. One of the largest American settlements was at Sacramento. To the Mexicans, the American settlers were helping them colonize their vast land. Many Americans, however, were led more by their desire for rich land than by any wish to help the Mexicans.

"Catching wild horses on the prairies, Texas," artist unknown

THE REPUBLIC OF TEXAS

Within a few years, Mexico began to regret its invitation to the Americans. Many of them did not do as they had promised. They did not obey Mexican laws, become citizens, or give up slavery. Mexico had very few government officials in northern Mexico to enforce its laws. By 1835, 35,000 Americans were living in Texas.

In 1836, the Texans declared independence and raised an army. Mexican president Antonio López de Santa Anna led 3,000 Mexican troops to northern Mexico. His troops surrounded the Alamo, a small garrison of Texans at San Antonio. On March 6, 1836, Santa Anna's men stormed the Alamo and killed 183 defenders.

A few weeks later, the commander of the Texas forces, Sam Houston, defeated Santa Anna at the San Jacinto River. The victors declared Texas a republic and elected Houston as its first president.

Antonio López de Santa Anna (1795?–1876)

Texas remained a republic for ten years. Then the United States annexed it and made it the twenty-eighth state of the union.

THE MEXICAN-AMERICAN WAR

Mexico bitterly resented the loss of Texas. Tensions remained high between Mexico and the Republic of Texas for years. When the United States annexed Texas, Mexico broke off diplomatic relations with the United States. Mexico claimed that the border between it and the new American state ran along the Nueces River. The United States, however, claimed the border was at the Rio Grande River, many miles farther south.

Many Americans wanted to fulfill a dream of "Manifest Destiny," or the U.S. occupation of all the land from the East to the West coasts. They approved of going to war with Mexico to gain further territory. Some Americans, including Abraham Lincoln, disapproved of the idea. But in May 1846, American troops marched into Mexico and captured the capital. They soon subdued Mexican troops in California, Arizona, and New Mexico. After another year of fighting, the Americans defeated the Mexicans and won the war.

The Treaty of Guadalupe Hidalgo Early in 1848, Mexican and American agents signed a peace treaty in the town of Guadalupe Hidalgo near Mexico City. Mexico recognized Texas's annexation and gave up much other territory. This included the land where the states of California, Arizona, Nevada, New Mexico, Utah, and parts of Colorado and Wyoming now exist. The land, known as the Mexican Cession, amounted to 500,000 square miles.

In return, the United States agreed to pay Mexico $15 million plus $3 million in war damages. A few years later, the United States purchased another 30,000 square miles of southern Arizona for $10 million. This land was for a railroad. This purchase was known as the Gadsden Purchase. Except for Alaska, it was the final territory on the continent to be annexed by the United States.

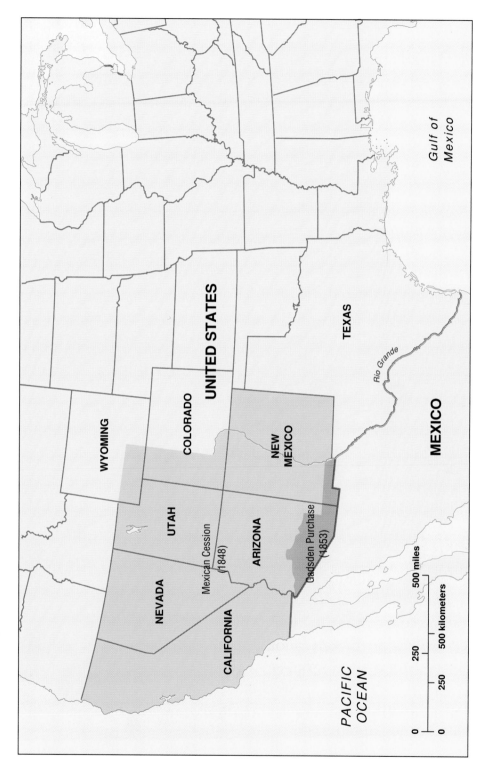

Area acquired from Mexico by the Mexican Cession (1848) and the Gadsden Purchase (1853)

MEXICAN AMERICANS IN THE ANNEXED LANDS

Suddenly, 80,000 Mexicans found themselves residents of the United States. The Treaty of Guadalupe Hidalgo guaranteed them the right to move to Mexico or to remain and become American citizens. Most chose to stay. Only about 3,000 returned. The treaty also guaranteed those who remained all the rights of American citizens.

Although the land now belonged to the United States, Mexican Americans were in the majority in California, New Mexico, and Arizona. Only in Texas did Americanos outnumber Mexicanos. However, many Mexican Americans lived in San Antonio, Laredo, El Paso, and Brownsville.

The numbers soon changed. Gold was discovered in northern California in 1849. That brought hundreds of thousands of people from all over the United States and the world to northern California. Americans also began to move into Arizona when the transcontinental railroad was completed in the 1870s. By the 1880s, the majority of the population was English speaking. Thousands of Texans also moved west to New Mexico. However, New Mexico's population remained largely Spanish speaking until after New Mexico became a state in 1912.

Outcasts in Their Own Land   Although they were the original settlers, the Mexican Americans in the annexed lands found themselves in a poor position. They were a minority of the population. They spoke a different language, they looked different, and they followed different customs.

The Stolen Land Grants   Many Mexican Americans in the Southwest lost their property and wealth after the Mexican-American War. Most of the landowners had received their lands as grants from the Spanish and Mexican governments. The Treaty of Guadalupe Hidalgo promised them the rights to

**A Mexican *vaquero,* or early cowboy on the ranges
of Texas and New Mexico, by Frederic Remington
(1861–1909), artist of the American West**

A street in El Paso, Texas, 1885

their lands. However, the federal government made the landowners go to court to prove they possessed Spanish land grants for their lands. The whole process deliberately favored the English-speaking newcomers. For the average Mexican American landowner the process took seventeen years. It also was very expensive. Many landowners had to borrow money to protect their claims. Very few won their cases. Some of those who did had to sell their lands to pay their debts. Thousands of once-proud landowners became poor ranch hands, sheepherders, or farm workers.

Discrimination and Abuse Most of the Mexican Americans of the Southwest were mestizos. Their brown skins, Spanish language, and Catholic religion marked them as different. To many Americanos, they were non-whites and therefore inferior. Americanos believed Mexican Americans were lazy and hot tempered.

Mexican Americans were treated as second-class citizens. Many were prevented from voting, except in New Mexico, where they remained in the majority. Law-enforcement officers, such as the Texas Rangers, treated them very harshly. They were often arrested on the slightest pretext.

Some states enacted laws that discriminated against Mexican Americans. In California, for example, foreigners had to pay a special tax to dig for gold during the gold rush. Californios also had to pay the tax, even though they were natives of the state. In some cases, Americano mobs murdered, lynched, or robbed Mexicanos for the slightest offenses.

In various parts of the Southwest, Mexican Americans tried to resist the all-powerful Americanos. In California, for example, a well-known folk hero, Joaquin Marietta, fought back. Mexican Americans saw him as a hero. Americanos saw him as a bandit.

IMMIGRATION, 1848–1900

Perhaps 100,000 immigrants came to the Southwest from Mexico during the second half of the nineteenth century. The economy in Mexico was very poor. There were few jobs. In addition, the farmlands of northern and central Mexico were poor. People had a hard time raising the food their families needed.

Thousands of Mexicans went to California to try to strike gold and get rich in the gold rush of 1849. These included many skilled miners from Sonora in northern Mexico. Most of them did not get rich, but they found jobs in mines throughout the West.

Many Mexican immigrants went to work picking cotton, herding sheep and cattle, and raising crops in Texas. Others went to southwestern cities, such as Tucson and Los Angeles, to find work. By 1900, there were about 500,000 Mexican Americans. About 400,000 had been born here. Another 100,000 had emigrated from Mexico.

Mexican revolutionaries, November 1913

Mexican Immigration, 1900–1940

WHERE THE MEXICANS CAME FROM

Between 1900 and 1940, 750,000 Mexicans immigrated into the United States. Some of them came from the northern part of Mexico, but most Mexican immigrants came from the central plateau. They came from the states of Jalisco, Guanajuato, and Michoacán. In those states, most people were poor, uneducated farmers. Many had become deeply indebted to merchants and landowners.

Why the Mexicans Came   The Mexican immigrants came to America for two reasons. First, they hoped to escape their grinding poverty. There were few jobs in Mexico, but the American economy was booming. The immigrants found well-paying jobs in mines, on railroads, in factories, and on farms all over America.

The immigrants also came to escape the violence of war and revolution. In 1910, civil war broke out in Mexico. The rebels succeeded in overthrowing Porfirio Díaz, the dictator, but the war lasted for more than ten years. Mexican government troops destroyed villages and massacred thousands of peasants. They believed the peasants were loyal to the rebels. Between 1910 and 1921, many Mexicans fled to the United States to escape the war.

MEXICAN IMMIGRATION
1900–1939

1900–1909	31,200
1910–1919	185,300
1920–1929	498,900
1930–1939	32,700

Source: Stephan Thernstrom, ed. *Harvard Encyclopedia of American Ethnic Groups.* (Cambridge: Harvard Univ. Press, 1980), p. 699.

This table shows the steady growth in Mexican immigration in the twentieth century until it was interrupted by the Great Depression of the 1930s.

Legal and Illegal Immigration Before the Great Depression of the 1930s, it was very easy for Mexicans to come to the United States. To immigrate legally, they each had to pay an eight-dollar tax and pass a medical examination. After 1917, they also had to pass a literacy test in Spanish. Despite these relatively easy requirements, many people could not qualify. Some did not have the money for the tax. Others could not read or write, even in Spanish.

For those who could not meet immigration requirements, it was still easy to come to the United States. The Immigration Act of 1924 imposed quotas on people coming from many countries in Europe and barred most people from Asia. But there were no quotas for people coming from other nations in the Western Hemisphere. The government did not try to stop people from crossing back and forth across the border. Mexicans came and went rather freely. If they could not meet the immigration requirements, many just immigrated "informally" by walking across the border.

WHERE THE MEXICANS WORKED

Railroads   Many Mexicans who came to the United States in the first three decades of the 1900s went to work for the railroads. They worked as maintenance and construction laborers, car cleaners, stock loaders, and in yard gangs. By 1930, Mexican Americans made up 75 percent of the labor force on six of the largest western railroads.

Industry and Service Jobs   Many immigrants went to work as unskilled laborers on construction projects, as pick and shovel miners, or as maids and gardeners. Others got jobs in steel mills, in meat-packing plants, and in textile mills. For the most part, Mexican and other immigrants did the most dangerous and unpleasant jobs in these industries.

Agriculture   Many Mexican immigrants became migrant workers. They moved around the country following the harvest seasons. They took jobs that had been filled by Asians who could no longer come to the United States.

The Mexicans were willing to work for low wages. They were also willing to perform backbreaking stoop labor.

The migrant laborers followed the growing season from one place to another. They picked fruits and vegetables in California, cotton in Texas and Arizona, and sugar beets in Michigan and Colorado.

Here is how one Texas farmer described his Mexican workers in the 1920s:

> *The Mexicans are a wonderful people; they are docile; I just love them. I was paying Pancho and his whole family 60 cents a day before the war (World War I). There were just no hours; he worked from sun to sun.*

As quoted in Matt S. Meier and Feliciano Rivera, eds., *Readings on La Raza* (New York: Hill and Wang, 1974), p. 68.

WHERE THE MEXICANS LIVED

About 95 percent of the immigrants settled in California, Texas, and other parts of the Southwest. Los Angeles, Tucson, and San Antonio attracted many Mexican Americans. A few went to Chicago to work in the railroad and meat-packing industries. Many worked in the steel mills and settled in Gary, Indiana, and Pittsburgh and Bethlehem, Pennsylvania. Some also went to Detroit to work in automobile factories.

Like other immigrants, Mexican Americans tended to settle in groups. Many moved into *barrios,* or "neighborhoods," in the poorest sections of town. Railroad workers and their families lived together near the railroad yards in company-owned camps called *colonias.* Two or three hundred people would make up a colonia. Migrant workers were housed in work camps at each farm or ranch where they worked for the season.

Happy in their own groups, Mexican Americans could speak their own language and have family and friends nearby. They felt less threatened by discrimination and violence in their own

Crowded conditions in the barrios in the 1930s caused health problems. This Mexican American woman and her children are being interviewed by a visiting nurse in San Antonio, Texas, in 1936.

This view of a barrio in San Antonio was taken in 1939 or 1940. Many Mexican Americans had to live in such poor conditions at that time.

neighborhoods. Also like other immigrants, they often had no choice about where they lived. Most immigrants were usually very poorly paid. They could not afford anything better than the shacks, camps, and colonias for their families.

THE BARRIOS

The earliest barrios grew up in Los Angeles, San Antonio, and other southwestern cities. At first, they were shantytowns on the edges of the cities. One or two families would build rough shacks without toilets or running water. Then relatives, friends, or fellow workers would build their own houses nearby. Gradually the barrios would grow and expand outward, becoming part of the city. One of the oldest and largest Mexican American barrios is East Los Angeles.

Traditionally, Mexican Americans have large families. They also tend to live together in extended families. Grandparents, parents, and children all live in one house. These large families made the barrios very crowded. With so many people living together in such close quarters, disease became commonplace. Many people suffered from tuberculosis in the barrios before World War II.

Barrio Life   Living in the barrios was not all bad. By living together as they did, Mexican Americans were able to preserve their culture while learning to speak English and to pick up "American" customs. They continued to speak Spanish and taught their children Spanish. They did not lose their native language as many other immigrant groups had. They had their own churches, social clubs, and newspapers. Their families and the clubs provided help and support when they needed it.

Many Mexican Americans became small-business owners. They operated barbershops, restaurants, shops, grocery stores, and funeral parlors in the barrios. The residents of the barrios enjoyed their traditional Mexican foods, holidays, music, and pastimes. All these things helped make life easier for them in the United States.

Mexican Americans in California. These future U.S. citizens celebrate the end of their classes in citizenship that prepared them for their naturalization examinations.

DISCRIMINATION

Mexican Americans continued to suffer from discrimination throughout the twentieth century. Many other Americans continued to regard them as inferior.

Most Mexican Americans could only get jobs that whites did not want. Often, they were paid less for doing the same job as other workers. If they tried to move out of the barrios, they often could not buy homes in white neighborhoods. Many house deeds included language that said an owner could sell a house to "Caucasians [whites] only."

Segregated Schools Most Mexican American children went to segregated, all-Mexican schools. The segregated schools were usually not as good as white schools.

In Texas, Mexican Americans were required to use separate facilities reserved for them and blacks. These included separate sections of theaters and trains, restaurants, and hotels.

MIGRANT LABOR

Working conditions were wretched for Mexican migrant laborers. They performed backbreaking stoop labor all day long in the hot sun after they were recruited by a labor contractor or "patron" to work for a particular farmer. Wages were always low and the hours always long. In the 1920s, a Mexican laborer would earn ten cents an hour or less. A typical migrant worker would work twelve hours a day and take home ninety cents for a day's labor.

The workers lived in rough barracks. Most did not have running water or sanitation. Most of the migrants were men. In some cases, whole families worked in the fields. The children could not go to school very often because they were needed in the fields. Two or more families often lived together in one room at the labor camps. Sometimes the rooms were so crowded that people had to sleep in shifts.

Migrant laborers move from place to place, working long hours. These Mexican Americans are picking cotton in Coachella Valley, California, ca. 1930.

The migrant laborers were transported from place to place in uncomfortable, dangerous trucks. In the 1930s, labor contractors sent migrant workers from Texas to Michigan in open trucks to pick beets. They sat crowded together on planks for hundreds of miles. Here is how one writer described the trucks:

*The average (truck) carries about fifty
people, their bedding and equipment and
food for the trip. Once the Mexicans have
crowded into the back, a heavy tarpaulin is
thrown over them and fastened down
around the edges so they are concealed.
Outwardly the truck looks as though it were
loaded with a cargo of potatoes. . . . The
truckers drive like devils. With a relief driver
in the cab, they go straight through to
Michigan, stopping only for gas and oil. By
driving night and day, they can make the
trip in from 45 to 48 hours.*

As quoted in Wayne Moquin, ed., *A Documentary
History of the Mexican Americans.* (New York:
Praeger, 1971), p. 312.

LABOR ORGANIZING

When they first started coming to America, Mexican American workers had a reputation for being docile. Business and farm owners believed that Mexicans would work for less money than others and that they would not form unions. Some business owners used Mexican workers to break union strikes. Some unions would not accept Mexican Americans as members. Some unions required Mexican Americans to present naturalization (citizenship) papers before they could join. There were no such requirements for persons born in Europe or Canada.

Despite their reputation for being gentle, Mexican American workers were often in the forefront of organized labor activities. As early as 1883, Mexican American *vaqueros* (cowboys) led a strike for better pay in Texas. If they could not join other unions, the workers formed their own.

Between 1900 and 1930, Mexican Americans led or took part in several miners' and railroad workers' strikes. Some 500 Mexican American track workers led a strike of Los Angeles electric railways in 1903. A few years later, in 1915, 5,000 miners—70 percent of them Mexican Americans—successfully struck the copper mines in Arizona.

Mexican American workers were also involved in organizing farm workers during the Great Depression in the 1930s. They formed more than forty agricultural unions. The farm labor unions staged several strikes for higher pay and improved working conditions. The growers would harass the strikers and have them arrested. The owners would even hire men with clubs to beat them up.

THE GREAT DEPRESSION

In 1929, the American stock market crashed. Thousands of businesses went bankrupt. The country entered the period of the Great Depression. At the same time, a terrible drought dried up farmlands in parts of the Midwest and Southwest for several years. Millions of people lost their jobs, their farms, and their homes in the depression.

America no longer needed the cheap labor provided by Mexican and other immigrants. White Americans now wanted the immigrants' jobs. Bankrupt farmers from Oklahoma, Arkansas, Texas, and other states flooded into California looking for work.

In addition, some 8,000 Chicano farmers lost their farms. Many other Chicanos lost their jobs to other workers. Before the depression, only 20 percent of migrant workers were whites. By 1936, white workers held 85 percent of all farm jobs.

New immigrants were no longer welcome. It became much more difficult for Mexicans to obtain visas to come to America than ever before. In all of the 1930s, only 32,700 Mexican immigrants received visas. The U.S. Border Patrol began to search for illegal immigrants and to deport them.

TAKING A TRAIN TO MEXICO

As the Great Depression continued, many Americans began to demand that immigrants be sent back to their native countries. There were no jobs for them. They were also using up government relief funds. The federal government started a repatriation program to send Mexican immigrants back to Mexico.

The program was supposed to be voluntary. But in some cases, people were picked up if they simply looked Mexican. They were placed on trains and shipped to Mexico City. The Southern Pacific Railroad Company transported Mexicans back to Mexico for $14.70 each.

An estimated 300,000 to 500,000 people were sent back. As many as half of them may have been American citizens. Some citizens were deported because they did not get a chance to prove their citizenship. Others were children who did not want to be separated from their deported parents.

For citizens and immigrants alike, the repatriation program was a cruel measure. Some Mexicans were able to work on public works projects started by the Mexican government. Others simply returned to extreme poverty. The program separated families and emptied barrios. It forced many Mexican American businesses to close. It took years for the Mexican American community to recover from repatriation.

Mexican Americans served with distinction in the armed forces during World War II. Here, being sworn in, is the first Mexican American to be commissioned as a navy nurse.

World War II and Mexican Immigration, 1940 to the 1990s

WORLD WAR II

The United States went to war in December 1941. The war put an end to the Great Depression. Millions of young Americans, including Mexican Americans, were drafted into the military. Suddenly, defense plants offered hundreds of thousands of new jobs making tanks, planes, and guns. Some Mexican Americans, including many women, were able to get jobs in the defense plants. Most, however, were hired back by farmers and ranchers.

Even during the war, Mexican Americans suffered from discrimination. Many defense plants and other industries would not hire them. The reason, the plant owners said, was that "Americans will not work with Mexicans."

DISCRIMINATION AND OPEN CONFLICT

The worst example of discrimination against Mexican Americans occurred in 1943 in Los Angeles. The case was called the "Zoot Suit Riots." Zoot suits were the fad at the time. They had baggy pants with tight ankles and long jackets with wide shoulders. Mexican American teenagers who wore them called themselves *Pachucos* after a town in Mexico. They began to refer to everybody else as *Anglos*.

Sailors on leave from their ships hired taxis and searched Los Angeles for all the Mexican Americans they could find. They were especially looking for young men dressed up in zoot suits. The sailors beat up the Mexican Americans while the police did nothing to stop them. The newspapers blamed the Pachucos. Twenty-seven were arrested before the violence ended. Clearly, a war was also being fought on the home front.

MEXICAN AMERICANS IN THE ARMED FORCES

Despite the prejudice and discrimination they suffered, Mexican Americans were eager to serve their country during World War II. More than 350,000 Chicanos served in all branches of the armed forces. Soldiers and sailors earned seventeen congressional medals of honor, the nation's highest award for valor. That was more than any other minority group.

Most Mexican Americans were placed in mixed military units with Anglos. This enabled them to make friends with Anglos and learn about American culture. One group of soldiers, Company E of the 141st Regiment, was made up of Spanish-speaking Mexican Americans from El Paso, Texas. They were sent to Italy and fought with valor.

One of the most outstanding Mexican American soldiers was Guy Louis Gabaldon. Gabaldon had grown up with Japanese American foster parents and knew how to speak Japanese. He was sent to fight the Japanese in the Pacific Islands. Several times, Gabaldon walked into the jungle by himself and talked Japanese soldiers into surrendering by calling out to them in Japanese. He is credited with capturing more than 1,000 Japanese soldiers!

Returning Home When Mexican American soldiers returned to the United States after the war, they came back with a new attitude. They felt they had served their country well and deserved to be treated with respect in return. Many took advantage of the G.I. Bill of Rights. This law provided veterans, people who had served in the armed forces, with money to go to college or buy a home. One group of Mexican American veterans formed the G.I. Forum, an organization to help Chicanos obtain their rights as citizens.

THE BRACERO PROGRAM

The war created a labor shortage in the United States. Farmers did not have enough workers to harvest their crops. The railroads did not have enough workers to run the trains.

The governments of the United States and Mexico started the bracero program in 1942. *Bracero* meant a person who worked with his or her arms (*brazos* in Spanish). Under the terms of the program, Mexicans agreed to come to work in the United States, then return home. By the time it ended in 1947, the bracero program had brought 200,000 workers from Mexico to the United States. Most worked as migrant farm laborers. About 80,000 worked for the railroads. After the program ended, the United States sent the braceros back to Mexico. Some stayed on illegally or soon returned to continue to work as migrant laborers.

In 1951, the Korean War caused another farm labor shortage. The bracero program was started up again. It continued until 1964. At the height of the program in 1959, 450,000 braceros came to the United States. In 1960, they made up one-fourth of all American farm workers.

Braceros harvesting broccoli in Texas

The "Undocumenteds" After World War II, about 30,000 Mexicans a year immigrated legally into the United States. Altogether, about 274,000 legal Mexican immigrants came to America in the 1950s. More than 440,000 came in the 1960s. Many hundreds of thousands more came illegally. Because there are no records of them, no one knows the exact numbers.

Illegal Mexican immigrants are commonly called "undocumenteds" because they do not have visas or citizenship papers. During the 1950s, they also came to be called "wetbacks." "Wetback" is a derogatory term. It refers to illegal immigrants who wade across the Rio Grande River to enter the United States.

Both legal and illegal immigrants came for the same reasons as earlier Mexican American and other immigrants to the United States. Most people in Mexico still lived in poverty. Mexicans could earn far more money in the United States than in Mexico. In the 1940s, farm workers in Mexico earned only sixty-five cents a day. As braceros in the United States, they received fifty cents an hour. Although that seemed like a lot of money to a Mexican laborer, it was much less than American farm owners had to pay Anglo workers.

Illegal immigrants wade across the Rio Grande.

LA MIGRA

During the 1950s, the U.S. government decided that the flood of illegal Mexican immigrants had to be stopped. The U.S. Immigration and Naturalization Service (INS) began to step up enforcement of immigration laws. The Mexican immigrants called the INS *La Migra*. Undocumented immigrants always lived in fear that La Migra would catch them and deport them to Mexico.

Controlling the Border   The job of the INS and the border patrol is to prevent illegal immigrants from crossing the border into the United States. That has proved to be an almost impossible task. Much of the 2,000-mile border passes through empty deserts and mountains. There are hundreds of roads and trails that people can use to enter the United States illegally.

Immigrants gather in towns just across the Mexican border and wait for the chance to cross into the United States. For many years, families would just wade across the river and walk into America. Now, most hire "coyotes," guides who take them across and supply them with false papers. Today, a coyote can get $700 to $1,500 per person for a border crossing and papers. In a few cases, coyotes have taken truckloads of people across the border and abandoned them in the desert to die. In some places, people cross the border by gathering in a group of several hundred and just running across. They know the border patrol will catch some but others will make it.

In 1955, the INS launched "Operation Wetback" to capture and return illegal immigrants to Mexico. INS agents would sweep through restaurants, barrios, and factories. They would arrest every Mexican who could not prove citizenship or legal residence. In 1960, the INS captured 60,000 illegal immigrants. In 1964, the number was 82,000. In many cases, the same people were caught and sent back again and again.

THE NEW IMMIGRANTS

By the 1960s, America's Chicano population appeared to fall into three categories—longtime citizens and residents, commuters, and illegal immigrants.

Longtime Citizens Mexican Americans are longtime citizens if they have been in America for generations. They have lived in the barrios for years and have worked steadily in a variety of blue-collar jobs. Some are moving into the middle class and into white-collar occupations. Their children are becoming Americanized. Many have intermarried with Anglos. Five out of six still speak Spanish at home, but almost all of them can speak English.

Commuters Commuters are Mexicans who are legally allowed to enter the United States to work. They hold "green cards." The cards identify them as legal aliens. They also serve as government work permits that allow them to get jobs. Thousands of these workers live in Mexican border towns such as Tijuana and Ciudad Juárez. They cross the border every day to work. Then they return to Mexico at night. In Ciudad Juárez, 13,000 commuters go to jobs in the United States every day. Most of these workers are women. They work as housekeepers and baby-sitters for American families.

Illegal Immigrants Most new immigrants are illegal or undocumented immigrants who still come to work in the fields and factories. Many commute seasonally and have been doing so for years. Many of them are men. They come to make money, not to settle in the United States and become citizens. Most stay an average of six to eight months at a time. Undocumenteds work for the lowest wages in terrible working conditions. Their employers know that they cannot complain. If they do, they will be discovered and deported.

Many Mexican Americans and other Americans resent the undocumented immigrants. As they see it, the "illegals" keep wages low and take jobs from Americans. Undocumented immigrants also strain social services such as schools, hospitals, and welfare. On the other hand, undocumented immigrants pay taxes and Social Security. They spend money in the United States and take jobs that no one else wants.

MOVING TO THE CITIES

Mexican Americans have been moving from rural areas to the cities steadily throughout the twentieth century. After World War II, they began moving to urban areas at a much faster rate. In the 1920s, half of all Mexican Americans lived in cities. In the 1950s, about two-thirds of the Chicano population had moved to the cities. By 1980, 85 percent had.

When they moved to the cities, they also changed jobs. Gradually, fewer and fewer Mexican Americans worked on the farms, and more took jobs in factories, stores, and offices. In the 1930s, two-thirds of all Mexican Americans worked on farms. Only 13 percent did by 1970, and the percentage continues to decline.

According to the 1980 U.S. Census, most Mexican Americans continue to live in California (3.6 million) and Texas (2.8 million). Six other states—Illinois, Michigan, Washington, Florida, Indiana, and Ohio—also have large Mexican American populations. Many of these people moved to Chicago, Detroit, and other cities to work in industries such as steel and automobile manufacturing.

Street scene in a Los Angeles barrio

MOVING UP

Life improved for many Mexican Americans after World War II. The G.I. Bill enabled many veterans to go to college and move into white-collar jobs. Mexican Americans began to fight discrimination and prejudice. They formed political groups to back candidates who were sympathetic to their problems.

By 1980, more than 1.4 million Mexican Americans worked in professional and management jobs. Several thousand had become doctors, lawyers, and teachers. Others had become clerical workers and salesclerks.

More and more Mexican Americans started their own businesses. Most are small businesses that serve the Chicano community. These include stores, restaurants, barbershops, and other services. One of the largest Chicano businesses is a savings-and-loan bank owned by the East Los Angeles Community Union. This bank makes loans to other Mexican Americans so that they can start their own businesses.

Despite these gains, most Mexican Americans still work in unskilled labor, service, and farm jobs. They are still wielding picks and shovels, working as maids and waiters, and laboring in the fields.

The incomes of Mexican Americans have improved, but they still lag behind those of whites and most other minority groups. In 1987, the median annual income for Mexican American families was $19,970. The median income for white families was $32,270.

Many Mexican Americans remain poor. The U.S. Census Bureau reported in 1986 that more than one out of four Hispanic families fell below the federal poverty line. (The poverty line is calculated each year by the federal government. Families whose annual income falls below that level are officially classified as poor. For example, in 1986 the poverty level for a family of four was $11,203.) The unemployment rate is also higher for Mexican Americans than for most others.

THE 1965 IMMIGRATION ACT

In 1965, the federal government enacted a new immigration law. The new law set a limit of 120,000 immigrants per year from the Western Hemisphere and 170,000 from the Eastern Hemisphere. The new law was a great benefit to many immigrant groups. It meant that many more Chinese, Japanese, and Filipino immigrants could come to the United States.

After the new law was enacted, illegal immigration skyrocketed. In 1965, the INS deported 105,000 Mexicans. In 1972, it sent back 505,000, and in 1973, 655,000 went back. The number deported represented only those who got caught. According to some estimates, for every one illegal immigrant who was caught, three were not.

Some experts estimated that there were perhaps 1 million to 2 million illegal Mexican aliens in the United States.

MEXICAN IMMIGRATION 1940–1980	
1940–1949	56,200
1950–1959	273,800
1960–1969	441,800
1971–1980	640,300

Sources: Figures for 1940–1969 taken from Stephan Thernstrom, ed. *Harvard Encyclopedia of American Ethnic Groups.* (Cambridge: Harvard Univ. Press, 1980), p. 699. Figures for 1971–1980 taken from *World Almanac.*

This table shows the steady increase in legal Mexican immigration through 1980.

Unions organize a strike against California grape growers in 1965.

THE CHICANO MOVEMENT

The civil rights movement of the early 1960s had a profound effect on Mexican Americans. Like blacks, Mexican Americans had been barred from using public facilities such as restaurants and hotels. Like blacks, they often had to send their children to inferior, segregated schools. And like blacks, they could not live and work where they pleased.

Mexican Americans began fighting for their rights in a variety of ways. They formed political groups, took segregated school districts to court, marched on college campuses, and organized labor unions. Until this time, some Mexican Americans had considered the term *Chicano* derogatory and insulting. Now, Mexican American civil rights activists adopted it to identify themselves. It expressed their pride in their Mexican heritage. They also called themselves *La Raza,* Spanish for "the people."

The Chicano movement tried to deal with many problems. These included discrimination, work, housing, and people's civil rights. One group even tried to get back the Spanish land grants in New Mexico. One of the movement's major aims was to improve the education of Chicano children. Like the black civil rights movement, the Chicano movement was successful in removing the worst injustices. However, much remains to be done.

THE 1965 GRAPE BOYCOTT

In 1965, two farm labor leaders, a Filipino American named Larry Itliong and a Mexican American named Cesar Chavez, organized a major strike against California's grape growers. Their workers were making less than $2,000 a year. They worked ten to twelve hours a day and lived in squalid labor camps. They had no health or unemployment insurance.

The strike was an outgrowth of the Chicano movement. It began in Delano, California, the heart of the state's grape-growing industry. It lasted five years and involved 17,000 seasonal farm workers. Before the strike was over, Itliong's and Chavez's unions combined to become one large, powerful group, the United Farm Workers Organization.

Their unions called for a nationwide grape boycott. After the strike ended, it was estimated that 17 million people had boycotted grapes. Another 11 million had boycotted California wine. The strike was successful in winning better pay and conditions for the workers. It established the right of farm workers to organize and strike. It also gave the Mexican American farm workers a sense of pride and power that they had never felt before.

Cesar Chavez

Cesar Chavez was born on his family's farm in Yuma, Arizona, in 1927. His parents lost their farm during the depression because they could not pay the taxes on it. The family members became migrant farm laborers.

Chavez joined the U.S. Navy in World War II and served two years in the Pacific fighting the Japanese. After the war, Chavez settled in San Jose, California. In the 1950s, Chavez became a community organizer. Many of the people he helped were farm workers. Chavez became convinced that the best way to help them was to organize a farm workers' union.

In 1962, Chavez moved to Delano and began organizing. The union opened a health clinic and started a theater. It helped the workers in applying for citizenship, registering to vote, and obtaining loans and welfare.

Chavez started the grape strike in 1965 with less than 2,000 workers. Today the union has more than 100,000 members. Chavez still leads the United Farm Workers.

EDUCATION

Mexican American children have not done as well in school as whites and some other minorities. Many of them drop out before finishing high school. In Los Angeles, the dropout rate for Mexican Americans reached 68 percent in the late 1970s.

Mexican Americans have not done well educationally for many reasons. For many years, they were relegated to second-rate, segregated schools where they received inferior educations. The children of migrant workers were always changing schools. They would fall behind in their schoolwork. Then they would get discouraged and quit.

Many Mexican American students tested poorly on intelligence tests. They had not been taught the language and culture well enough to score higher. But the schools assumed that they were stupid. Instead of being encouraged to go to college, they were placed in vocational classes. They were told that they should "learn a trade."

Bilingual Education   Many people believed that one way to help immigrant children was to teach them school subjects in their own language. In 1968, President Lyndon Johnson signed the Bilingual Education Act. *Bilingual* means "two languages." The new law was intended to help school districts start bilingual education programs. The schools would teach immigrant students in their own languages. They would also provide special English classes so that the students could gradually learn English.

The program really did not get started until about 1978, when Congress provided more money for it and required that the law be enforced. Most of the students who received bilingual education were Spanish speaking. In 1981, a government report estimated that about 1.4 million students needed bilingual education.

However, opinions are divided about how well the program works. Some Americans believe that children should be taught in English if they are going to succeed in America. Others are convinced that bilingual education has helped Spanish-speaking children to learn and has kept them in school longer.

Today, the federal government spends about $140 million a year on bilingual education. That is only about one-fourth of what is needed to carry out the program. But most school districts still offer bilingual education.

Mexican American children bash piñatas at a Christmas fiesta,
Market Square, San Antonio, Texas.

Mexican Americans Today

LIFE IN THE PRESENT

What is life like for the roughly 12 million Mexican Americans today? Some things have not changed very much. Most people remain crowded into the barrios in many cities. We hear a great deal about illegal immigrants, but more than four out of five Mexican Americans were born in the United States.

As a result of the Chicano movement and school desegregation, more Mexican Americans are going to college today than ever before. Many colleges have established departments of Chicano studies so that Mexican American students can learn about their own culture and history.

Despite having long had a reputation for fighting, drinking, and breaking the law, Mexican Americans form stable families. Furthermore, studies have shown that the crime rate in Chicano barrios is no higher than that in other neighborhoods.

About 95 percent of Mexican Americans are Catholics. Religious holidays have great importance. Most holidays are celebrated with fiestas, music, food, and dancing. On Christmas and birthdays, adults fill papier-mâché figures called *piñatas* with candies. Then the children take turns hitting the piñata. When it is broken, they all scramble for the treats.

LANGUAGE

Mexican Americans have been able to preserve much of their culture. In addition to the 12 million Mexican Americans in the United States, about 7 million other Spanish speakers are here. All of these people together are called "Hispanics."

More than 2 million Puerto Rican Americans and about 1 million Cuban Americans are the largest of the other Spanish-speaking ethnic groups. Hispanic people have migrated into every state of the union. Two-thirds of them live in California, Texas, and New York.

Many, if not most, Hispanics speak Spanish at home. All except the very newest arrivals can and do speak English. Living together in barrios has made it easier for people to continue to speak Spanish. Spanish has also had an important impact on American life. Many of the place names in the American West and Southwest are Spanish. Los Angeles, El Centro, Nogales, Las Cruces, and Del Rio are just a few. The early Spanish settlers named their towns after Catholic saints. Today, many of those towns are large cities, such as San Francisco, San Jose, and San Antonio.

Spanish Words in English   Hundreds of Spanish words have entered the English language. The following Spanish words are just a few:

alligator	buffalo	castanet
chili	cigar	corral
desperado	fiesta	gala
gringo	guerilla	indigo
loco	machete	macho
mesa	mosquito	mustang
negro	peon	pinto
plaza	poncho	pronto
ranch	siesta	sombrero
stampede	tornado	vanilla

MEXICAN AMERICAN ORGANIZATIONS

A strong sense of community has helped Mexican Americans adapt to life in the United States. Chicanos, like many other ethnic groups, have always banded together to help one another. They have formed many clubs and organizations. Some are social clubs where they can gather for celebrations and family events. Others are groups formed to provide legal services, language and basic education classes, emergency loans, insurance services, and counseling. Many of these organizations provided money and leadership during the struggles of the Chicano movement. The League of United Latin American Citizens (LULAC) is one of the largest and best known of these groups. It was formed in Texas and led the fight during the 1960s to desegregate Chicano schools.

Press and Broadcasting Hundreds of Spanish-language newspapers, newsletters, and magazines serve Hispanic communities throughout the United States. *The Westside and Southside Sun* in San Antonio, Texas, has a circulation of more than 100,000. The *Hispanic Review of Business,* published in New York, is a magazine with a circulation of 125,000. Some popular American magazines also publish Spanish-language versions. *Harper's Bazaar* and *Popular Mechanics* are two of these.

There are also many radio stations throughout the United States that broadcast in Spanish. Several dozen television stations either broadcast all of their programming in Spanish or offer some Spanish-language programming.

All of these Hispanic organizations and media provide a great deal of information to Mexican Americans about culture, life, and laws in the United States. They also discuss Hispanics' rights and obligations as Americans. The groups and media also enable Mexican Americans to take pride in their own heritage and accomplishments.

POLITICAL POWER

For decades New Mexico had a tradition of electing Mexican Americans to high office. Two U.S. senators from New Mexico were Mexican Americans, Dennis Chavez and Joseph Montoya. The Chicano movement taught other Mexican Americans that they, too, must become involved in politics. Mexican Americans came to realize that they could change things if they use their power to elect or defeat political candidates.

In the 1960s, Mexican Americans in Texas formed La Raza Unida. This regional political party was made up of Mexican Americans. It started out by electing members to the city council in Crystal City, Texas. Soon it was affecting county and state elections as well. In 1981, the citizens of San Antonio, Texas, elected Henry Cisneros as the first Mexican American mayor of a large city.

The Mexican American vote has become very important to presidential candidates. During presidential elections, candidates make it a point to visit Hispanic neighborhoods and speak to Hispanic crowds. They are photographed attending a fiesta or eating tacos. Mexican Americans know that in the Southwest they have the numbers to make their votes count.

George Bush, candidate for president in 1988, campaigned for the Mexican American vote.

Paintings by Mexican American artists in East Los Angeles

MUSIC, ART, AND ARCHITECTURE

Mexican Americans influence our culture in many ways. Music is very important in Mexican American life. Throughout the Southwest, traditional mariachi bands play Mexican music at fairs, parties, and fiestas. Songs range from sad love songs to lively dance numbers. In recent years, young musicians have blended traditional Mexican sounds with rock 'n' roll to create a new form of popular music called *salsa*.

Mexico has been producing outstanding artists since the days of the Mayas. Today, Mexican American artists combine folk art and vibrant colors to produce many beautiful artworks. Mexican American artists often work in murals. These are large pictures painted on walls. You can see murals done by Mexican American artists on the walls of public buildings throughout the Southwest.

Architecture   Go anywhere in the West and you will see the influence of Mexican architecture. Many homes and other buildings are constructed of adobe with red tile roofs. They are often decorated with colorful Mexican tiles and exposed beams. High ceilings and thick walls help the buildings stay cool.

Raul Castro

Raul Castro was born in a mining town in Sonora, Mexico, in 1916. He was one of fourteen children. His father, a miner, left Mexico during the Mexican Revolution of 1910–1921. The Castro family settled in a Mexican barrio near Douglas, Arizona. Raul's father died when Raul was twelve, leaving his family extremely poor during the Great Depression.

Castro struggled to learn English and go to school even though it was very hard for him. He graduated from high school in 1935 and worked his way through Arizona State College. After World War II, Castro studied law at the University of Arizona Law School.

Soon after he became a lawyer, Castro was elected as the county attorney for Pima County, Arizona. Later, he became a state superior court judge. In 1964, President Lyndon Johnson appointed Castro as the U.S. ambassador to El Salvador. His Hispanic background and ability to speak Spanish made Castro a popular ambassador in El Salvador. In 1968, President Johnson named him to be the ambassador to Bolivia. Castro returned to Arizona in 1969 and took up his law practice again.

Raul Castro rose from the most abject poverty to become his country's chief representative to two foreign governments. In addition, he enjoyed a reputation for being a fine international lawyer and an outstanding judge.

Linda Chavez

In the 1980s, when Ronald Reagan was president, Linda Chavez was the highest-ranking woman in the White House. She is a respected educator and public official who has held several important positions in the federal government.

Linda Chavez was born in 1947 in Albuquerque, New Mexico. When she was ten, her family moved to Denver, Colorado. She graduated from the University of Colorado with a degree in English literature. Later, she earned graduate degrees at the University of California and the University of Maryland.

In the 1970s, Chavez worked for two national teachers' organizations, the National Education Association and the American Federation of Teachers in Washington, D.C. President Jimmy Carter appointed her to a position in the U.S. Department of Health, Education, and Welfare in 1977.

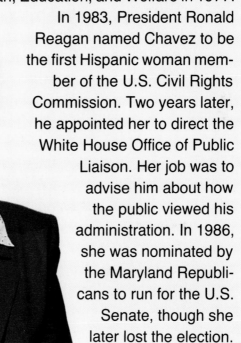

In 1983, President Ronald Reagan named Chavez to be the first Hispanic woman member of the U.S. Civil Rights Commission. Two years later, he appointed her to direct the White House Office of Public Liaison. Her job was to advise him about how the public viewed his administration. In 1986, she was nominated by the Maryland Republicans to run for the U.S. Senate, though she later lost the election.

José Arcadio Limón

José Limón was born in 1908 in Culiacán on the west coast of Mexico. Like so many others, his parents were forced to flee Mexico during the Mexican Revolution. They settled in southern California, where Limón attended The University of California at Los Angeles (UCLA) to study painting. He left California for the New York School of Design in the 1920s. As a painter, he was unsuccessful. Disappointed, he quit art school. But later Limón found the way to express his artistic talent. He enrolled in modern dance classes. Within two years, he was dancing on Broadway and was beginning to choreograph.

Limón's dancing career blossomed during the 1930s. He based his dances on Mexican themes. They were very popular with audiences all over America. During World War II, Limón served in the U.S. Army for two years. After the war, he resumed his work. Limón made several very successful foreign tours during the 1950s. He also taught dance at several universities and started his own dance company.

Limón died in 1972. He left sixty-nine modern dance compositions, among them *Danza de La Muerte* and *La Malinche.* Many of them are still performed. He is remembered for both the skill and the dramatic passion he brought to his dancing.

Joan Baez

Joan Baez is one of the best-known Mexican Americans in the United States. She has been a popular folk singer and political activist since the 1960s. Baez was born in Staten Island, New York, in 1941. Her father was a physicist and her mother a drama teacher. Baez learned to play the guitar when she was twelve. Although she was a Mexican American, she grew up not knowing how to speak Spanish.

In the late 1950s, the family moved to Boston. Baez began to visit the city's coffee houses and learn folk songs. She made her first public appearance as a singer at the Newport Folk Festival in 1959. Her beautiful soprano voice soon made her a popular performer. In the 1960s, Baez became active in the civil rights and anti-Vietnam War movements. Baez appeared for Cesar Chavez during the grape strike and marched with Martin Luther King, Jr.

Baez's singing career has been very successful. She has eight gold albums and many best-selling single recordings. Over the years, she has continued to lend her voice to various causes. In 1985, she appeared in the Live Aid concert to aid African famine victims. The following year, she took part in an Amnesty International concert tour.

Other Outstanding Performers Many Mexican Americans have excelled in music, the arts, theater, and athletics. Here are a few well-known Mexican Americans in each field.

In Music Two well-known Mexican American singers are Richie Valens and Linda Ronstadt. Valens was only seventeen years old and already had two hit records when he died in a plane crash in the 1950s. The movie *La Bamba* told the story of his life. Ronstadt grew up listening to her father, a mariachi singer, sing the songs of his Mexican homeland. Ronstadt has enjoyed a long career as a popular singer. A few years ago, she returned to her roots and produced an album of Mexican music. She called the album *Songs of My Father*.

The Arts Two of America's most outstanding Mexican American artists are Alfredo Mendoza Arreguin and Willie Herron. Arreguin has won many awards for his elaborate paintings of tropical plants and animals. The United Nations Children's Fund (UNICEF) chose one of his paintings for its Christmas card in 1985. Herron is a widely known muralist in California and the Southwest. He often chooses Aztec, Chicano, and Mexican themes for his colorful wall paintings.

In the Theater Anthony Quinn is the world's best-known Mexican American actor. Born in Chihuahua, Mexico, Quinn is perhaps most famous for his portrayal of Zorba the Greek in the theater and on film. Quinn has enjoyed a long career on stage and in the movies playing a variety of ethnic roles, including a role in the story of Mexican revolutionary Emiliano Zapata, *Viva Zapata!*

In Sports Former National Football League (NFL) quarterback Jim Plunkett is a Mexican American. Plunkett won the Heisman Trophy for best college football player in 1970. He led the Oakland Raiders to a Super Bowl win in 1981. A current Mexican American NFL superstar is Anthony Muñoz, of the Cincinnati Bengals. He is often voted the best offensive lineman in football.

Lee Trevino and Nancy Lopez are world-famous professional golfers. Both have won countless professional tournaments and hundreds of thousands of dollars in prize money. Trevino was elected to the American Golf Hall of Fame in 1981.

MEXICAN AMERICAN FOOD

Mexican food is very popular all over the United States today. Most people are familiar with tacos, chili, burritos, tamales, and enchiladas. Mexican restaurants have long been plentiful in the Southwest and California. Now, excellent Mexican restaurants can be found in every large city in America.

Many Mexican dishes come from the Indians who inhabited Mexico before Columbus. Imagine that you could go back into the past and stroll through an Aztec Indian village with Cortés. You would see Mexican women preparing tortillas, tacos, and tamales much as they do today.

Tortillas are flat, round pancakes made out of corn or wheat. Corn was the most important ingredient in Aztec cooking. Today, it is still the basis for most Mexican cooking. Many dishes, such as tacos and enchiladas, involve making a spicy filing for tortillas. In Mexican villages, you can still see women grinding corn on flat stones to make tortillas. They take a ball of dough, pat it flat, and then cook it in hot oil. In modern cities, cooks buy tortilla flour already ground. They use a tortilla press to flatten the dough.

Tortillas form the basis of this Mexican food spread.

Chilies and fruit add zest to Mexican cooking.

Ingredients in Mexican Cooking Mexico's Indians gave us many of the foods we enjoy today. In addition to corn, these include chocolate, vanilla, tomatoes, sweet potatoes, pineapple, and beans.

Mexican cooks use chilies, beans, and tomatoes in many dishes. Chilies are peppers. They spice and flavor many fillings and sauces. Most people think all chilies are very hot and spicy. In fact, chilies range from mild and sweet to very hot. Beans are usually served separately or mashed and fried. Tomatoes are used fresh or cooked in sauces.

The Spanish conquistadores also added many ingredients to Mexican cooking. They brought wheat, rice, beef, pork, chicken, milk, butter, oil, cinnamon, and peaches to the New World. Modern Mexican cooking includes many beef, pork, and chicken dishes.

Mexico also gave us one very popular cooking custom, the barbecue. In ancient Mexico, the Indians wrapped meat in cactus or banana leaves and roasted it in pits dug in the ground. The Spanish called this method of cooking *barbacoa*. Today, when we roast our meats on backyard grills, we, too, enjoy a barbecue.

58

THE 1986 AMNESTY ACT

In the 1980s, many people became concerned about illegal immigrants who entered the country without permission. Most of the illegal immigrants came from Mexico. Although the National Research Council reported from 1.5 million to 3.5 million illegal immigrants, some officials even talked about 12 million illegals "flooding" the country.

Some illegal immigrants had been here for many years. They had worked hard and been good members of the community. In 1986, Congress enacted an amnesty program. An amnesty is a kind of forgiveness or pardon. This allowed illegal immigrants who came forward and met certain requirements to remain in the country legally. Nearly 1.5 million people did so.

Congress also enacted new laws that make employers examine the identity papers of people they hire. Congress hoped that these laws and the amnesty program would finally solve the problem of illegal immigration. That has not happened.

The new laws fine employers who hire illegal aliens. This has led to much discrimination against Hispanics. Some employers will not hire people with Spanish names for fear they are illegal. Others charge Hispanic workers fees to cover the costs of possible fines. Even Hispanic American citizens have been turned down for jobs because of the new laws.

As long as wages and living standards are much higher in the United States than in Mexico, many Mexicans will cross the border with or without permission. Many who do so earn money here and go back to Mexico. They live in Mexico but work in the United States. Other illegal immigrants, as we have seen, stay here and raise families. If their children are born here, the children are citizens even though their parents are not.

PROBLEMS OF MEXICAN AMERICANS

Mexican Americans still suffer from old problems. Many people are still at the bottom of the economic ladder. Only one-fourth of Mexican Americans work in white-collar jobs, and few are skilled workers. The rest work in unskilled, service, and farm jobs. Mexican Americans are still among the lowest-paid workers in America. In 1987, the median annual income for Mexican American families was less than $20,000 compared with more than $32,000 for Anglos. As discussed in an earlier chapter, too many Mexican American children are dropping out of school and not receiving adequate educations. A 1987 study estimated that only about 45 percent of Mexican American adults were high school graduates.

Chicano Gangs　　One of the most serious problems in Mexican American and other urban communities is youth gangs. Many teenagers, both boys and girls, join gangs.

Gang members are fiercely loyal to one another. Each gang controls its own "turf." A gang's turf may be a several-square-block part of the barrio or as little as one block. The gangs adopt symbols to identify themselves. Each gang member usually has a nickname. The gang members paint their symbols and names on city walls. These graffiti are often very elaborate and colorful.

The Chicano and other ethnic gangs have long been a problem in cities with large barrios, such as Los Angeles. In recent years, however, the gangs have become very violent. Many are involved in selling drugs. They frequently go to war with each other for control of drug sales on their turf. Some gang members have acquired guns. Each year, hundreds of young people are killed in barrio gang wars. Many Mexican American and other families have lost their young people to gang violence.

THE FUTURE OF THE MEXICAN AMERICAN COMMUNITY

The 12 million Mexican Americans are part of one of the largest ethnic groups in the country. Despite continuing discrimination and poverty, their lives are clearly improving. Two members of President George Bush's cabinet, Lauro F. Cavazos (Education) and Manuel Lujan (Interior), are Mexican Americans. Others are climbing the ladders of political and economic success. Mexican Americans are beginning to vote in greater numbers and with more influence.

Since immigration from Mexico, both legal and illegal, is bound to continue, the Mexican American population will continue to grow rapidly. Since all Hispanic groups have a strong attachment to the Spanish language, the influence of that language will continue to grow. There are even people who fear that Spanish will displace English in some parts of the United States. But that is unreasonable. Mexican Americans, like most people in this country, work hard for economic and social advancement, and that advancement can only occur for those who have mastered English. The fact that millions of Americans speak more than one language can be a great advantage both to individuals and to the country as a whole. Mexican Americans have contributed to the past growth of the United States and will continue to do so in the future.

Mexican market, San Antonio, Texas

SOURCES

Bouvier, Leon, and David Simax. *Many Hands, Few Jobs: Population, Unemployment, and Immigration in Mexico and the Caribbean.* Washington: Center for Immigration Studies, 1988.

Daniels, Roger. *Coming to America: A History of Immigration and Ethnicity in American Life.* New York: Harper & Row, Publishers, Inc., 1990.

De la Garza, Rodolfo O., et al., eds. *The Mexican American Experience.* Austin: Univ. of Texas Press, 1985.

Ehrlich, Paul R. *The Golden Door: International Migration, Mexico, and the United States.* New York: Ballantine Books, 1979.

Galarza, Ernesto, Herman Gallegos, and Julian Samora. *Mexican Americans in the Southwest.* Santa Barbara: McNally & Loftin Publishers, 1969.

Garver, Susan, and Paula McGuire. *Coming to North America: From Mexico, Cuba, and Puerto Rico.* New York: Delacorte Press, 1981.

Langley, Lester D. *MexAmerica: Two Countries, One Future.* New York: Crown Publishers, Inc., 1988.

Meier, Matt S., and Feliciano Rivera, eds. *Readings on La Raza.* New York: Hill and Wang, 1974.

Morin, Raul. *Among the Valiant.* Alhambra, Calif.: Borden Publishing Co., 1963.

Moquin, Wayne, ed. *A Documentary History of the Mexican Americans.* New York: Praeger Publishers, 1971.

Servin, Manuel P. *An Awakening Minority: The Mexican Americans.* Beverly Hills: Glencoe Press, 1974.

Thernstrom, Stephan, ed. *Harvard Encyclopedia of American Ethnic Groups.* Cambridge: Harvard Univ. Press, 1980.

Weyr, Thomas. *Hispanic America: Breaking the Melting Pot.* New York: Harper & Row, Publishers, Inc., 1988.

INDEX